W9-ACG-644

Stay Safe Online

Smartphone Safety

Eric Minton

PowerKiDS press

New York

Published in 2014 by The Rosen Publishing Group, Inc.
29 East 21st Street, New York, NY 10010

First Edition

Editor: Amelie von Zumbusch
Photo Research: Katie Stryker
Book Design: Colleen Bialecki
Book Layout: Joe Carney

Photo Credits: Cover jonya/E+/Getty Images; p. 5 Driendl Group/Photodisc/Getty Images; p. 6 iroha/Shutterstock.com; pp. 7, 9, 11, 13, 16, 29 iStock/Thinkstock; p. 8 Aman Ahmed Khan/ Shutterstock.com; p. 10 Ciaran Griffin/Stockbyte/Thinkstock; pp. 12, 21 Hemera/Thinkstock; p. 14 Dan Porges/Photolibrary/Getty Images; p. 15 Yellow Dog Productions/The Image Bank/Getty Images; p. 17 holbox/Shutterstock.com; p. 18 racorn/Shutterstock.com; p. 20 Hill Street Studios/Blend Images/Getty Images; p. 23 Aletia/Shutterstock.com; p. 24 Monkey Business Images/the Agency Collection/Getty Images; p. 25 Tetra Images/Getty Images; p. 27 Neil Beckerman/Photonica/Getty Images; p. 28 Bloomberg/Contributor/Getty Images.

Library of Congress Cataloging-in-Publication Data

Minton, Eric.
 Smartphone safety / by Eric Minton. — First edition.
   pages cm. — (Stay safe online)
 Includes index.
 ISBN 978-1-4777-2935-9 (library) — ISBN 978-1-4777-3021-8 (pbk.) —
 ISBN 978-1-4777-3092-8 (6-pack)
 1. Smartphones—Juvenile literature. 2. Mobile computing—Safety measures—Juvenile literature. 3. Internet and children—Juvenile literature. 4. Safety education—Juvenile literature. 5. Internet—Safety measures–Juvenile literature. I. Title.
 QA76.59.M56 2014
 004.167—dc23
                                    2013026848

Manufactured in the United States of America

CPSIA Compliance Information: Batch # W14PK2: For Further Information contact Rosen Publishing, New York, New York at 1-800-237-9932

Contents

Smartphones Are Cool! 4

The Downside of Smartphones 6

What's the Password? 8

Know Your Apps 10

Security Systems 14

On the Map 16

Taking Pictures and Videos 18

Bullying from a Distance 22

Oh No! I Lost My Phone! 26

Dial "R" for Recycling 28

Be Smart and Safe 30

Glossary 31

Index 32

Websites 32

Smartphones Are Cool!

A smartphone is a cell phone that can do many of the same things a computer can. Unlike other cell phones, smartphones can run computer programs called **apps**. These include **social media** apps, music players, and video games.

Your smartphone can connect to the Internet, allowing you to visit websites and send email. You can use it to keep in touch with friends and family. You can also get information like maps, bus schedules, sports results, and weather reports with it.

There are many smartphone models, such as the Motorola Droid and iPhone. Each has different features and different prices. Common features include a **touch screen**, a camera to take photos and videos, and a GPS for finding your way around.

Smartphones come in many different models. They are all useful for searching the Internet and staying in touch with people. They're fun to play games on, too!

Did You Know?

This year's fancy, expensive smartphone is next year's discount phone. Shop with your parents for a smartphone in your family's price range.

5

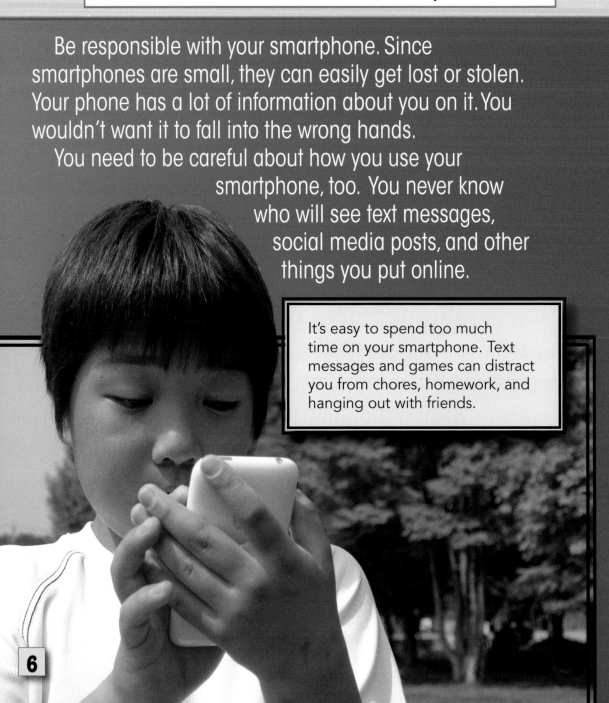

The Downside of Smartphones

Be responsible with your smartphone. Since smartphones are small, they can easily get lost or stolen. Your phone has a lot of information about you on it. You wouldn't want it to fall into the wrong hands.

You need to be careful about how you use your smartphone, too. You never know who will see text messages, social media posts, and other things you put online.

It's easy to spend too much time on your smartphone. Text messages and games can distract you from chores, homework, and hanging out with friends.

6

Your parents may set limits on how you use your smartphone. Talk to them about the rules you need to follow and how much time you're allowed to spend on the phone.

Once you have sent or posted things, you often can't take them back. If you send someone a text or other private message, she can forward it to other people. If you regret a social media post and go back to delete it, someone may already have copied it.

What's the Password?

Bad things can happen if your smartphone gets lost or stolen. Whoever has it can read your private messages and send texts that look like they're from you. He can ruin your progress in your games. He can even erase your contact information and spend money from your bank account.

When you're in public, hide your screen whenever you type passwords or other private information. Don't let anyone else see what you type.

If you lend a friend your smartphone to play a game on, enter the password or PIN before handing it over. Don't just tell the other person the PIN or password.

Keep strangers from using your smartphone by going into your phone's settings to create a **password** or PIN. "PIN" is short for "personal identification number." Don't use an obvious PIN or password, such as "1234," "password," or your own name. If it's easy to guess, it won't protect your phone. Never show anyone your password or PIN. Even a friend might thoughtlessly share it with someone else or use it to play pranks on you.

Did You Know?

Don't use a password for your smartphone that you also use elsewhere. If you do, someone who learns that password can break into everything you've protected with it.

9

Know Your Apps

Apps are computer programs that run on smartphones or tablets. To start an app, touch the app's **icon** on your touch screen. The owner's manual or an online instructional video can tell you how to start an app on a smartphone without a touch screen.

There are thousands of different apps out there. Some apps tell you the weather forecast. They help you be prepared for whatever weather the day brings.

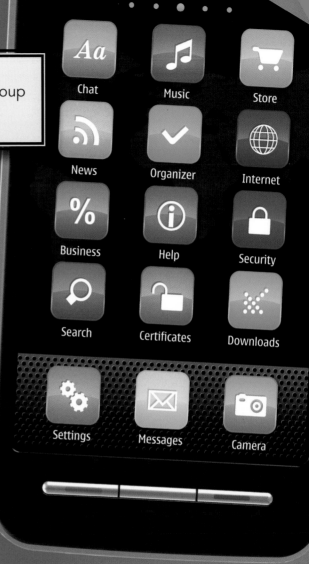

This smartphone uses icons to group apps by the kind of app they are.

You can download apps from a trustworthy app store, such as Google Play or the Apple App Store. Apps from other sources may contain computer **viruses** that can steal or erase phone numbers or other information. Other apps can increase your phone bills or interrupt phone calls.

If you download a dangerous app, erasing it may not fix things. If your phone still has problems, you'll have to erase everything on your phone with a **factory reset**.

Many apps cost money. You can get others for free, but some of these free apps have hidden costs. It is easy to spend a lot of money in some games to get special items or bonuses. Often there are so many things to buy that getting them all costs more than buying another game would. Other games let you play the first few levels for free and then make you pay for the rest of the game.

There are many apps that let you listen to music. Some are free and some are not. Before picking one, do some research and discuss the options with a parent.

Before you download an app, read online reviews of it to see if it has any hidden costs or if it is easily attacked by viruses.

Always check with your parents before you buy or spend money on an app. They can help you find bargains and steer you away from inappropriate, unnecessary, or dangerous apps.

Did You Know?

Some online games are designed so that you get stuck and can't make progress unless you spend extra money buying things in the game. Don't get tricked!

13

Security Systems

Security software apps protect your phone from computer viruses, hackers, and **spam** emails. Without them, you're more likely to lose time, money, and important messages and files. When you get a new smartphone, download and install good security software before you get any other apps.

Spam filters put messages that look like spam in a separate folder. If a friend's emails don't show up in your inbox, check the spam folder. Some emails end up there by mistake.

Antivirus software compares new apps, websites, and links to a list of known threats and blocks anything it recognizes as a virus. Spam filters recognize unwanted emails and remove them from your inbox.

Security software isn't foolproof. The designers of antivirus programs and spam filters can defend only against things they've seen. This means that brand-new threats may slip past your security software. **Update** your security software regularly to defend against new threats.

Have a parent or other trusted adult help you set up antivirus software on your smartphone. It can be tricky to do on your own.

Did You Know?

Never give out your name, home address, passwords, or other private information to strangers. No security software or password can protect your phone against this kind of attack.

15

Many smartphones include a global positioning system, or GPS, which shows exactly where you are on a map. You can use this to get directions if you're lost or going somewhere unfamiliar. Your parents can also use it to find you if you need help.

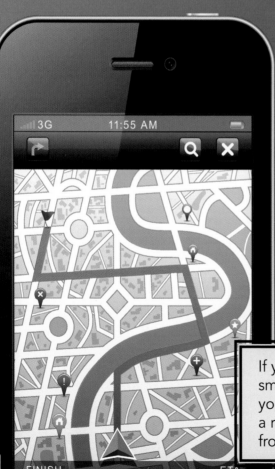

While your smartphone's GPS is turned on, the photos you take can contain hidden information on where you took them. This is called geotagging. Hackers can read geotags to see where you've been.

If you are taking a trip, your smartphone can show you where you need to go. It can even show a route you can use to get there from your present location!

If you get lost, a smartphone with GPS can show you where you are on a map.

Make sure your phone shows your location only when you need it to. You don't want strangers to be able to use it to find you. Go to the Location Services part of your phone's settings and turn GPS off when you don't need it.

Many smartphones have built-in cameras. You can use an app to take photographs or make videos. These are stored on your phone as computer files. A stand-alone digital camera may take nicer pictures, but your smartphone's camera is more convenient. It lets you attach photos and videos to emails and text messages. It also lets you post photos and videos on social media sites.

Think about safety when posting images. It can be dangerous to post photos and videos of yourself or other kids because it can help **Internet predators** find targets. This includes photos that don't show kids directly but provide information about them, such as pictures of someone's house or school. If you want to share photos with family or friends, make sure to do so privately.

18

If you want to share a photo with a friend, you could email it to her. You could also use a photo-sharing site that lets only people you approve see your photos.

Once you put photos or videos online, it can be impossible to get rid of them completely. Others can forward or link to embarrassing images over and over. There's no surefire way to guess if posting something will make people unhappy. If you take someone's picture, always get his or her permission before you post it and delete it if asked.

Photos can keep family members who live far away aware of concerts, games, and other important events. Just make sure to share the photos privately.

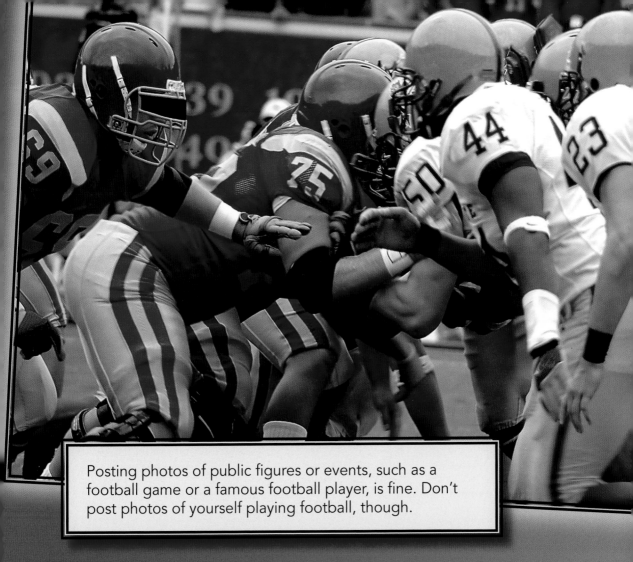

Posting photos of public figures or events, such as a football game or a famous football player, is fine. Don't post photos of yourself playing football, though.

On social media sites like Facebook, you can **tag** a photo or video so it appears when people search for the names of the people it shows. Some sites let you adjust your settings so the tag appears only if you approve it. While this keeps your name off a photo you don't want seen, it doesn't keep the photo itself from being posted.

Cyberbullying is any kind of bullying that happens online rather than in person. It happens in emails, text messages, and social media posts. It can include teasing, spreading rumors, revealing secrets, and making threats. Taking and sending embarrassing pictures or videos is also cyberbullying. Shutting someone out of an online group is, too. Pretending to be someone else online to give him a bad name is cyberbullying. Tricking someone into thinking you're someone else online can be, too.

Cyberbullying is as bad as any other kind of bullying. Never post anything that might hurt someone's feelings. It's important not to join in when your friends bully someone. If you find out someone is being bullied online, tell your parents and teachers.

If you have been getting bullying texts or emails from a cyberbully, try to block that person. Many email and texting programs allow you to block other users.

If you're the target of cyberbullies, remember that it's not your fault. It's okay to go to adults for help. Don't respond to the bully because what some bullies want most is to see that you're upset. Never bully them back or get into a fight. It's still bullying even if you have a reason. Adults may blame you for it.

Cyberbullying can make you feel scared and alone. Don't blame yourself, though. Nobody deserves to be cyberbullied.

Talking to a parent or other trusted adult about being cyberbullied can make you feel better. Adults can also help you find ways to stop bullies.

Always talk to a trusted adult if you're bullied online. Be sure to save every bullying message sent to you. Take a **screenshot** of every bullying social media post. Keep copies of these messages and screenshots in case your smartphone is stolen or hacked. You can make printouts or save the information on a personal computer, flash drive, or file-hosting service.

Did You Know?

Kids targeted by cyberbullies reported that changing their passwords, user names, email addresses, or phone numbers helped end the bullying. Deleting their social media profiles helped, too.

Be careful with your smartphone. Don't leave it lying around. Always check that you have it whenever you leave a place where you used it. Never take out your phone any place you feel unsafe.

If you do lose your smartphone, you can use a computer or another smartphone to find your missing phone using GPS. You can also erase everything on it to make sure that no one can see your private messages and photos. Some phones, like those with Apple iOS or Microsoft Windows, have such apps built in. For other phones, you'll need to download the right apps.

Set up your password and security apps sooner rather than later. It's too late to do so after your phone is lost or stolen!

You don't want to lose your smartphone. Smartphones are fun and very useful. They're also quite expensive.

Dial "R" for Recycling

When you get rid of an old smartphone, you never know who might get hold of it. Copy all the information on your smartphone that you want to keep, then do a factory reset to erase everything. Different phones have different ways to do this. Call your phone company's customer service line for more information.

This man works for a company that finds uses for old smartphones and other old electronics. Some are taken apart so parts can be reused. Others are reworked and resold.

When you get a new smartphone, you usually can get the people you are buying it from to transfer information from your old phone to the new one.

Like all computers, smartphones contain poisonous chemicals. If you throw yours in the trash, these materials leak into our soil, water, and air. Recycle it through an electronics recycling organization instead.

Owning a smartphone is a big responsibility. This starts when you pick one out and doesn't end until after you dispose of it. Always be careful about who uses your smartphone, where you put it, and what you do with it.

Did You Know?

Ordinary recycling services that handle paper, metal, plastic, and glass can't recycle electronics. Don't throw your old phone in an ordinary recycling bin.

Be Smart and Safe

1. Develop good smartphone habits. Always know where you've put your phone. Never leave it lying around in public.

2. Always update your phone's operating system when a new version comes out. Updates have new features and are harder for viruses to attack.

3. Make sure your parents write down your smartphone's identification numbers. They will need to give these numbers to the police if the phone is stolen.

4. Be careful when using public Wi-Fi hotspots. Change your phone's settings so it doesn't automatically connect to Wi-Fi.

5. If an app asks for permission to see your contact list or location, say yes only if there's a good reason to allow it.

6. Brand-new computer viruses can get past even the most up-to-date security software. Always think before you click on a suspicious link.

7. If your phone is stolen, use a computer to change all your email and social media passwords right away.

Glossary

apps (APS) Computer programs made for mobile devices, such as smartphones and tablets.

cyberbullying (SY-ber-bu-lee-ing) Doing hurtful or threatening things to other people using the Internet.

factory reset (FAK-tuh-ree REE-set) Clearing the information from a device so that it becomes like it was when it was first made.

icon (EYE-kon) A picture or image that stands for something.

Internet predators (IN-ter-net PREH-duh-terz) People who try to take advantage of kids they meet online.

password (PAS-wurd) Letters or numbers used to get access to an account.

screenshot (SKREEN-shot) A picture of what is on a computer screen.

social media (SOH-shul MEE-dee-uh) Having to do with online communities through which people share information, messages, photos, videos, and thoughts.

spam (SPAM) Unwanted email messages.

tag (TAG) To put a label or name on something.

touch screen (TUTCH SKREEN) A screen that you can touch to make a computer do things.

update (UP-dayt) To change something to make it more up-to-date.

viruses (VY-rus-ez) Programs that harm a computer.

Index

A
app(s), 4, 10–15, 18, 26, 30

C
computer, 4, 25–26, 29–30
cyberbullying, 22

E
email(s), 4, 14–15, 18, 22

F
factory reset, 11, 28
family, 4, 18
features, 4, 30
friend(s), 4, 9, 18, 22

G
game(s), 4, 8, 12

H
hackers, 14, 16

I
icon, 10
information, 4, 6, 8, 11, 16, 18, 25, 28
Internet predators, 18

M
map(s), 4, 16
models, 4
music players, 4

P
password(s), 9, 26, 30
programs, 4, 10, 15

S
screenshot(s), 25
social media sites, 18, 21
software, 14–15, 30

V
virus(es), 11, 14–15, 30

W
websites, 4, 15

Websites

Due to the changing nature of Internet links, PowerKids Press has developed an online list of websites related to the subject of this book. This site is updated regularly. Please use this link to access the list:
www.powerkidslinks.com/sso/phone/